A partnership between American Library Association
and FINRA Investor Education Foundation

FINRA is proud to support the American Library Association

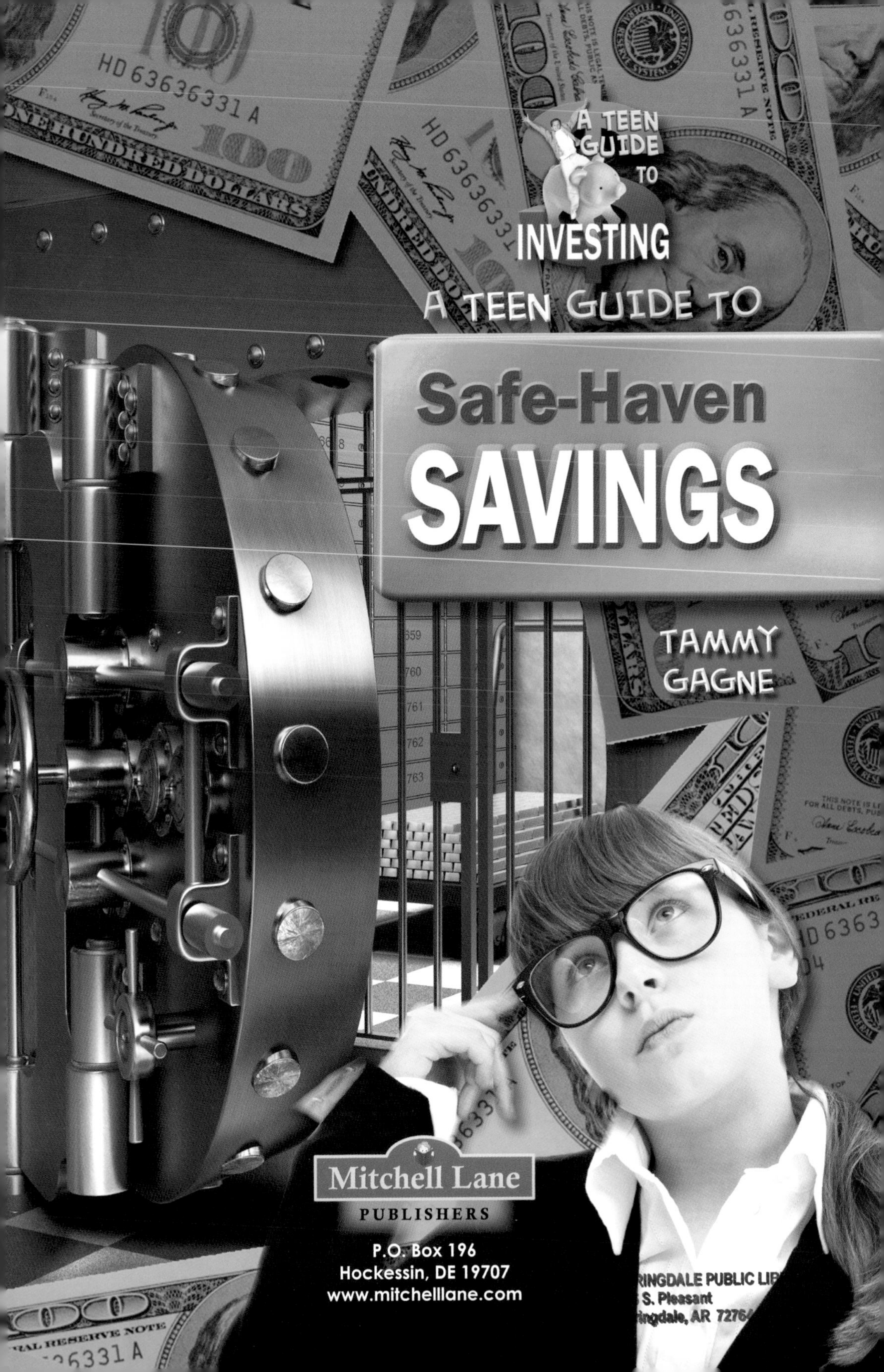

A TEEN GUIDE TO INVESTING

A TEEN GUIDE TO

Safe-Haven
SAVINGS

TAMMY GAGNE

Mitchell Lane
PUBLISHERS

P.O. Box 196
Hockessin, DE 19707
www.mitchelllane.com

A TEEN GUIDE TO INVESTING

Investment Options for Teens
A Teen Guide to Buying Stocks
A Dividend Stock Strategy for Teens
A Teen Guide to Buying Bonds
A Teen Guide to Buying Mutual Funds
A Teen Guide to Safe-Haven Savings

Printing   1   2   3   4   5   6   7   8   9

Library of Congress
Cataloging-in-Publication Data
Gagne, Tammy.
 A teen guide to safe-haven savings / by Tammy Gagne.
    pages cm.—(A teen guide to investing)
 Includes bibliographical references and index.
 Audience: Grade 7 to 8.
 ISBN 978-1-61228-428-6 (library bound)
 1. Savings accounts—Juvenile literature. 2. Investments—Juvenile literature. 3. Finance, Personal—Juvenile literature. I. Title.
 HG1660.A3G34 2014
 332.1'752—dc23
                                          2013012548

eBook ISBN: 9781612284903

                                          PLB

Contents

The Bank of England is one of the oldest banks still in existence today.

CHAPTER 1

A Penny Saved . . .
EARNS INTEREST

Saving money and investing money often go hand in hand. But not all investments are safe places for your hard-earned money. People who buy stocks, for instance, can earn a great deal of money on their investments. In rare cases, they can even become rich overnight. They can also lose every cent that they invested in just a single day. Because of this risk, many people prefer to invest most of their money in safe-haven savings.

Safe-haven savings are investments that offer little risk to the investor. Some people think that safe-haven savings aren't worth the time or money it takes to invest in them. If you take some time to learn about your options, however, you can earn a little at a time on your cash—without ever risking a penny of it.

The concept of a savings bank began during an era called the Age of Enlightenment. During this time period, people began to move away from spirituality and towards thought and reason for

The painting *Salon de Madame Geoffrin* depicts a gathering in an eighteenth-century-France salon, or drawing room. Social gatherings like this one were common during the Enlightenment in Europe. The most sophisticated members of society would assemble to share their thoughts and ideas about the new age.

guidance in their daily lives. This new way of thinking had an enormous effect on both religion and science. It also changed the way economics and politics worked. The middle class began to help less fortunate people by teaching them how to help themselves. They taught the poor about the importance of preparing for the future. Those in the middle class knew that putting money away today was the best way to plan for unexpected expenses tomorrow.

The first savings bank opened its doors in Hamburg, Germany, in 1778. Tottenham, England, followed when it opened the United Kingdom's first savings institution in 1798. Over the next century, other European countries opened their first banks as well. But people were not going to trust a bank with their hard-earned money without a good reason. What was the advantage of keeping money in a bank account instead of at home? The answer was interest—banks paid people to keep their money in savings accounts. The exact amount they were paid depended on how much money they kept in the bank. The more money a person deposited, the more interest that person would earn.

By itself, money isn't really worth anything. Money is just paper and metal. It is the items that these paper and coins can buy that give money its value. That value can actually change over time, and frequently money loses value because of inflation. Inflation is an increase in the cost of products and services. This can happen for many reasons, but most agree that it is affected by the money supply (how much money a government prints), and by the growth of the economy. An item that costs $1 one year could cost $1.25 the next. By keeping your money at home, your $1 is still worth $1 after a year. In the bank, your $1 earns a little extra money over one year, allowing you to buy more of the things that you need. Even if the cost of an item you need goes down, earning interest on your money from a bank will leave you with more money after you buy that item.

Over time, many people realized that saving was as good for society as it was for the individual. Banks could use the money that people kept in their accounts to make loans to people who needed money. People who wanted to buy property or open businesses could borrow the money from a bank. Banks charged interest on these loans. People who borrowed money paid a higher interest rate, and the bank paid out a slightly lower interest rate to the people who put their money in savings accounts with the bank. The difference (spread) allowed banks to make a profit so they could make additional loans to other people. People who bought land or businesses could borrow more money, which they used to make more money. They could then put more money in the bank. This cycle made both the banks and the people wealthier. Everyone was learning how to make their money work for them, instead of simply working for their money.

Because banks were becoming such an important part of society, governments soon got involved in establishing savings banks. To this day, governments play a large role in many countries' banking systems. Governments help manage interest rates. They also provide loan programs for people who may have a difficult time getting loans from a private bank. While some people think that government shouldn't be involved in the banking process, others believe that countries couldn't operate as well as they do without this relationship. When the economy is good, the government can help make it better by granting more loans. When the economy is bad, the government can stop things from becoming worse by denying loans to people who are poor credit risks. These are people who are less likely to be able to pay back their loans based on their income or past payment history.

The government can also control interest rates; in the United States, the Federal Reserve was created in part for this purpose. The Federal Reserve lends money to banks throughout the country, and decides at what interest rate that money will be loaned. When the banks loan that money to consumers, they lend it at a higher interest rate than the rate they pay to the Federal Reserve. When consumers deposit money, the bank will pay a slightly lower interest rate than what they pay the Federal Reserve. Controlling interest rates also helps the government to regulate the economy. When rates are high, more people will save their money because they can earn interest quickly, and fewer people will borrow money. With low interest rates, people are more likely to borrow money, since it is less expensive to do so.

You might be wondering if there are risks involved in keeping your money in a bank. For instance, what happens if your bank is robbed? What if there is a fire and your bank burns down with all of your money inside the building? What happens if your bank goes out of business? In the United States, your money will always be safe as long as you choose an FDIC-insured bank. The FDIC, or Federal Deposit Insurance Corporation, is an independent agency of the United States Government that has protected money held in US banks since 1934. According to

Some banks protect their money by keeping false stacks of cash with dye packs inside. When these stacks are stolen, a remote control can activate the packs to explode. The discoloration makes it impossible for the thieves to spend the cash without drawing attention to themselves. This stack of 20-dollar bills was abandoned after a robbery at a Bank of America for this very reason.

the FDIC, "no depositor has ever lost even one penny of FDIC-insured deposits."

It isn't just savings accounts that the FDIC insures. Checking accounts, money market accounts, and certificates of deposit (CDs) are also fully insured. The FDIC insures each depositor for up to $250,000 per bank. However, the FDIC does not insure investments in stocks, bonds, mutual funds, annuities, or life insurance policies—even if these investments are sold by a bank. It also doesn't insure items that are kept in safe deposit boxes.

One FDIC bank is just as safe as any other, but you will find that each bank is a little different. Nearly all banks charge fees to customers for the various accounts they offer. For example, one bank may charge you a higher fee for using automatic teller machines (ATMs) than another will. Some banks charge fees for maintaining checking accounts

London actor Reg Varney is best remembered as the star of the British sitcom *On the Buses*. On June 27, 1967, he became known for something else. Varney was the very first person in the world to use an automatic teller machine (ATM). The historic event took place at Barclays Bank in Enfield, United Kingdom.

while others may charge no fee at all. Comparing fees and finding the right bank for you can help you keep more of your money.

Different banks also offer different interest rates to their customers. This is how banks compete for business. One bank might pay more interest on savings accounts than another, but this same bank might charge a higher rate for loans than other banks do. It is important to shop around for the best bank for your needs. If your goal is to save money, choose the bank that offers you the highest interest rate on your deposits and charges the lowest amount of fees.

INVESTOR TRIVIA

The first chartered savings bank in the US was the First Bank of the United States. It was created by the United States Congress in 1791. Although the bank isn't operational anymore, you can still see the original building in Philadelphia, Pennsylvania.

One way to avoid many fees and earn a high interest rate is to deposit your money with a credit union. Credit unions are a lot like banks. They offer savings accounts, checking accounts, and investment programs just like a bank. They often call these accounts something slightly different. For example, many credit unions call a savings account a share account. A checking account is often called a share draft account. Despite the different names, these accounts work the same way as their bank counterparts. Credit unions are not-for-profit organizations, meaning that their primary goal is to help their members, not make a profit. Because of this, they can usually offer loans and investment opportunities to their members at better rates than most banks.

Credit unions have been around a very long time. Friedrich Wilhelm Raiffeisen opened the first institution of this kind in Neuwied, Germany, in 1846. Much like credit unions of today, Raiffeisen's rural credit union offered members the opportunity to save and borrow money with reasonable terms.

If you want to keep more of your hard-earned money, consider depositing it with a credit union. These alternatives to banks offer the same benefits but with lower fees. Credit unions are owned by their members, not big corporations like most banks.

The biggest difference between credit unions and banks is their size. Credit unions are owned by their members instead of by large companies. This may mean that a credit union has fewer locations than a large bank, which might make it more difficult to manage your money. Today, many credit unions are forming associations or alliances to give their members more options. These groups of different credit unions allow members to do their banking at the location of any credit union that is part of the group. Associations are making the list of differences between credit unions and banks smaller and smaller.

You won't be able to join just any credit union. These institutions have requirements for membership. The good news is that most people can find a credit union that will accept them. Most cities, towns, or counties have at least one credit union that allows anyone who is a resident of that community to join. Other credit unions are part of businesses, but you don't necessarily have to work for the business to be eligible to become a member. Oftentimes you simply need to be the relative of an employee to become a member yourself. Some credit unions are for students and faculty of colleges and universities. Others are for members of the military and their families. You are almost sure to find a credit union that will welcome you--and more importantly, save you money.

INVESTOR TRIVIA

Thanks to the FDIC, your money is safe in your savings account today. People who had deposited money in the Clay County Savings Association in Liberty, Missouri, back in 1866 weren't so lucky. This was the first bank that Jesse James ever robbed. He made off with almost $60,000 in bonds, gold, silver, and cash on February 13.

A piggy bank is a great place to save your loose change. But large amounts of money are safer in a bank.

CHAPTER 2

Banking
ON IT

Depositing your money in an FDIC-insured savings account is one of the safest things you can do with your cash. If you want your savings to grow as much as possible, however, it is important to do a little research. Each type of savings institution offers its own advantages. Likewise, different companies may offer different benefits. One type of savings account may also work better for you than another.

Both banks and credit unions offer statement savings accounts. Even certain credit card companies and insurance companies now offer this type of account to their customers. These accounts are usually the simplest form of savings. But because they don't offer much interest, many people prefer other investments. It may still be worthwhile to have one of these accounts, though—if you choose it wisely and use it to its fullest advantage.

Statement savings accounts typically offer the lowest interest of any type of investment. Each bank offers its own interest rate, but the difference may not be large. Depending on how much money you save, the difference between one account and another could be as little as a dollar or even less over the course of a year. But if someone were to hand you a dollar bill, what would you do with it? You might stuff it into a piggy bank. You might put it in your pocket. You might even forget that it's there. What you probably won't do is throw it away. If you choose an account with a low interest rate, however, giving up the extra interest is just like throwing that money away.

More often than not, credit unions offer the best interest rates, the lowest minimum balances, and the lowest account maintenance fees.

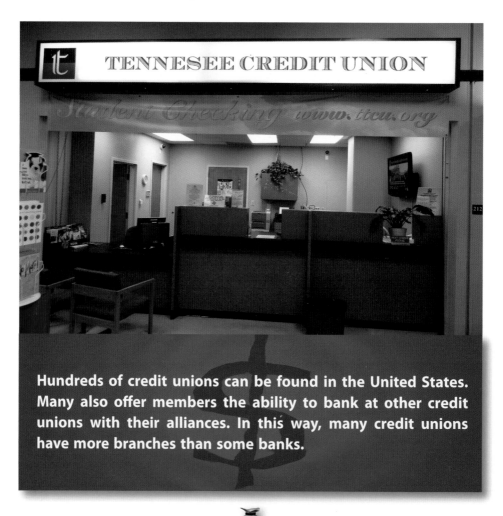

Hundreds of credit unions can be found in the United States. Many also offer members the ability to bank at other credit unions with their alliances. In this way, many credit unions have more branches than some banks.

Many credit unions require no minimum balance and charge no fees at all. The less you are paying in fees, the more of your money gets saved. The more money that gets saved, the more interest you will earn. If you are just beginning to save money, you may not have a lot of cash right now, but this can change over time. In the meantime, depositing money into a bank could actually chip away at your money instead of helping you increase it.

Let's say you have $100 to deposit into a statement savings account. If you open your account with a credit union that offers 2 percent interest, you would have $102 in a year's time. Now let's suppose you opened an account with a bank instead. The bank might offer you closer to 1 percent interest.* The bank is also more likely to require a higher minimum balance. If your bank charges a fee of $5 per month for accounts with balances of less than $500, by the end of that same year, you would have less than $41. You may think that no one would make such a foolish investment, but many people leave money sitting in accounts like these, not realizing that they are losing cash each month.

Most banks and credit unions send out regular statements to their customers. Statements list all the deposits, withdrawals, and interest earned. Most institutions provide checking account statements monthly, but savings account statements may only be sent quarterly. Either way, be sure to set up online access to your account. If you make a point of checking your balance regularly, you will be aware of any fees or errors as soon as possible.

In some cases, you might be able to save more money by going with a different type of financial institution. For example, if you have your driver's license, most states require you to purchase auto insurance. If you buy it from a company that also offers savings accounts, you

---

* Interest rates and fees discussed in this book are for illustration purposes only and may not be representative of actual rates or fees that are available at the time you are reading this book.

INVESTOR TRIVIA

You will need to bring identification with you when you open a new bank account. Bring your driver's license if you have one, but don't worry if you don't have this photo ID yet. A birth certificate and a social security card is usually enough identification for minors. You will, however, need an adult to sign the paperwork.

could earn a multi-product discount by opening both accounts with the same company. If you deposit the money you save on your insurance into your savings account, you could be saving even more money than you would with a credit union. Still, be sure to watch out for fees. Saving $20 a year on your auto insurance won't make up for losing $60 in account maintenance fees.

One of the best ways to limit account fees is by opening a children's savings account (CSA). Some banks offer CSAs to customers under eighteen years old as a way of introducing kids and teenagers to their companies. These accounts offer both lower balance requirements and lower maintenance fees than regular accounts. Many CSAs charge no fees whatsoever. A CSA may also offer other benefits, such as a rewards program. For example, you might earn a $25 savings bond once your balance reaches $500. Bear in mind that you may be required to maintain this higher balance. If you withdraw money after reaching that $500 mark, you could be charged for the bond. Also, some banks charge fees when a customer doesn't make deposits for an extended period of time. Many savings accounts have limits on the number of withdrawals that can be made in a single month.

One of the best ways to use a statement savings account is as a temporary place for your money. As long as your account has no minimum balance, you have nothing to lose and everything to gain by moving your money into another type of investment once your balance

Spending money can be fun, but watching your savings grow can be even more exciting. By saving money now, you will have more money to spend in the future. To help your savings grow as quickly as possible, choose an account that offers the highest interest and the lowest fees.

reaches a certain amount. If you want to keep the safety of a regular savings account while earning more interest, a money market account is a great option once you have saved enough cash. A money market account requires a larger minimum balance than most savings accounts, and in exchange it pays more interest than a regular savings account.

Minimum balances for money market accounts vary quite a bit from one institution to another. Again, a credit union may be your best option. A bank may require a customer to have $10,000 to open a money market account, but a credit union may only ask for a deposit of $2,500. Some credit unions even allow members to open a money market account with less than this amount (and no fees) and work their way up to earning higher interest. Don't assume that these money market accounts act like regular savings accounts until the balance hits the minimum amount, however. Most offer no interest at all until the

The more money you
save, the more interest
you can earn.

INVESTOR TRIVIA

In 2008, a company called SmartyPig combined the idea of a traditional savings account with social networking. When you open a SmartyPig account online, you begin by creating a financial goal. Perhaps you want to save for a cell phone, a laptop, or a car. Once you decide, you can then ask family members and friends to help you save for it, or share your goal progress through Facebook or Twitter.

balance reaches the minimum amount. If you don't have enough to earn the higher interest rate of a money market account, it is better to stay with the statement savings until you do. At this point, though, the amount of interest you can earn increases significantly. In general, you will earn the highest interest rates from money market accounts with the highest minimum balances.

Know the exact fees of a money market account before moving your savings into one of these high-yield accounts. Again, you are more likely to be charged a fee from a bank than from a credit union. Just like interest rates, though, fees can range quite a bit from one institution to another. As with savings accounts, many money market accounts limit the number of withdrawals owners can make each month, even if the minimum balance is maintained.

Even a low-interest money market account usually pays better than statement savings, but this isn't always the case. Although some savings accounts offer fixed rates that don't change, the interest rate can change with most savings and money market accounts. Your rate can go up or down with no notice whatsoever. Although there is a risk of losing interest, you also have the potential to gain interest. You will never, however, lose your original deposit or any amount of interest that has already been paid to you.

Before spending your cash, consider saving it instead. Saving just a dollar each day will add up to $365 in savings over a year—and that's before you add the interest you could earn on your money.

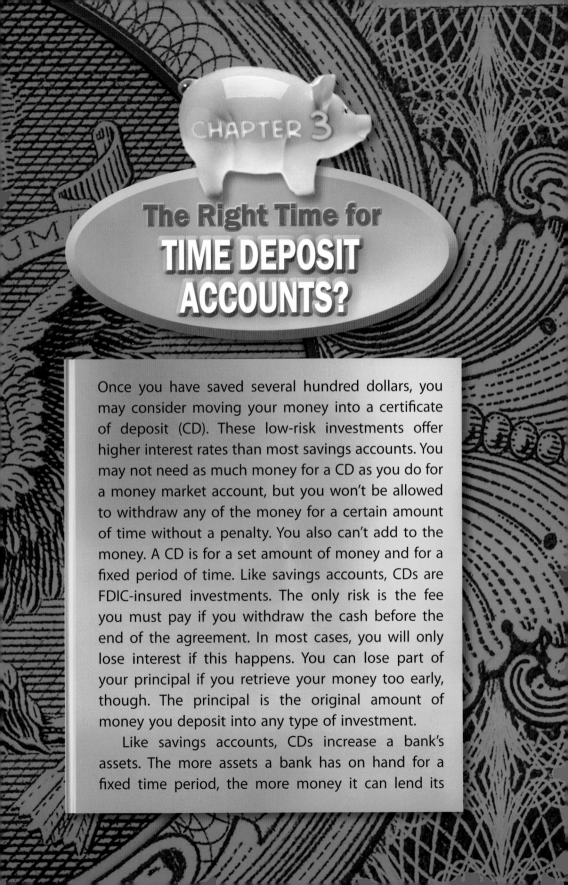

CHAPTER 3

The Right Time for
TIME DEPOSIT ACCOUNTS?

Once you have saved several hundred dollars, you may consider moving your money into a certificate of deposit (CD). These low-risk investments offer higher interest rates than most savings accounts. You may not need as much money for a CD as you do for a money market account, but you won't be allowed to withdraw any of the money for a certain amount of time without a penalty. You also can't add to the money. A CD is for a set amount of money and for a fixed period of time. Like savings accounts, CDs are FDIC-insured investments. The only risk is the fee you must pay if you withdraw the cash before the end of the agreement. In most cases, you will only lose interest if this happens. You can lose part of your principal if you retrieve your money too early, though. The principal is the original amount of money you deposit into any type of investment.

Like savings accounts, CDs increase a bank's assets. The more assets a bank has on hand for a fixed time period, the more money it can lend its

The United States Postal Savings System began January 1, 1911 and ended on July 1, 1967. During this time, post offices issued depositors savings certificates like the one pictured above from 1932.

customers. The bank can then make more money through the interest it charges on these loans. In the event that a customer withdraws money from a CD early, the bank also makes money from the penalty charged.

Also known as time deposit accounts, CDs have been around for several decades. The first CDs were issued in 1961. By the end of 1962, $6 billion worth of these time deposits were held by customers. The majority of these investments were held by corporate investors, or companies. About $2 billion worth of the CDs, though, were owned by

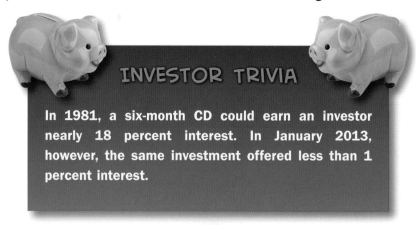

INVESTOR TRIVIA

In 1981, a six-month CD could earn an investor nearly 18 percent interest. In January 2013, however, the same investment offered less than 1 percent interest.

individual investors. By the late 1970s and early 1980s, CDs had become even more popular investments.

Like so many other investments, CDs offer far less interest today than they did in previous years. They may still be a wise investment choice for many people, though. One benefit to CDs is that they keep people from spending their money on an impulse. For example, your long-term goal might be saving for college. If you go shopping and see a great deal on a new laptop, you might be tempted to buy it if you have your money in a regular savings account. But with your money in

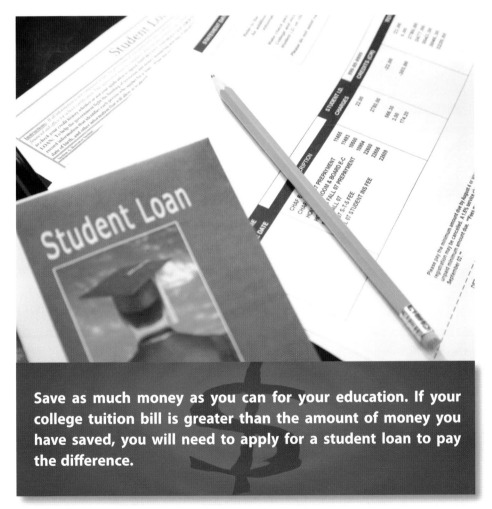

Save as much money as you can for your education. If your college tuition bill is greater than the amount of money you have saved, you will need to apply for a student loan to pay the difference.

Before spending money on a high-priced item, ask yourself if you will be glad you made the purchase a year from now. Electronics often cost a lot when you buy them, but they quickly lose their value following the purchase.

a CD, you may be less likely to buy the laptop because you will have to pay penalties as well. You could still end up buying a computer (or something else) when your CD matures, but in the time between now and then, you could also change your mind about the purchase.

CDs are available for different lengths of time, known as terms. You may opt for a three-month CD, a twelve-month CD, or even a five- or ten-year CD—or a term somewhere in between these time periods. The longer you are willing to leave your money in the investment, the better the interest rate will be. Unless you withdraw your money early, you won't lose any of the interest promised to you. You can, however, end up losing out on interest if you commit to a long-term CD and the rates rise after you invest your cash.

Banks have made certain changes to encourage people to invest in longer-term CDs despite the low rates. Investors now have the chance

Never be afraid to ask questions when you visit your bank. The tellers and other employees are there to assist customers like you.

to increase their rate on special CDs. Known as bump-up CDs, these investments generally offer lower rates in the beginning. If the going rate for a CD of equal length increases during the life of the investment, however, the CD owner has the option of bumping up to that higher rate. If rates do not increase, the owner only gets the original rate.

Different banks have different minimum amounts for CDs. You may need between $500 and $1,000 to purchase this type of investment, but many banks will open a CD with no minimum at all. If you have a large amount of money, it may be worthwhile to buy several smaller CDs instead of one large one. It may also be smart to choose CDs with various terms, a strategy called laddering. By choosing a variety of terms, you increase your chances of being able to reinvest your money when interest rates go up. You will also have your CDs maturing at various times, so you will have access to at least some of your cash on a regular basis, if you should need it.

CDs are frequently purchased through banks, but you can also buy these investments through brokers. Many people choose this option because brokered CDs usually offer higher interest rates than traditional bank CDs do. Both types of CDs are held by banks, but brokerage companies can afford to purchase these investments in significantly larger amounts. Because the brokers invest so much cash, the banks agree to give them higher interest rates. The brokers then break the CDs down into smaller amounts to sell to numerous individuals. One might say that brokers get a better deal because they buy in bulk.

Before placing your money in a CD (or any other type of savings account), ask for written information about the investment. This paperwork should clearly state the interest rate and any fees you could be charged.

One advantage of a brokered CD is that it can be resold to someone else, so you won't have to pay a penalty if you need your cash early. That doesn't necessarily mean you won't lose money, though. It all depends on where interest rates are when you need your cash. If they have dropped since you invested your money, you may not lose any of your interest. If they have gone up, though, you could end up losing some of your principal. Brokered CDs that come from FDIC-insured banks are insured just like bank CDs, but it could also take you longer to get your money if the bank that sold the investment goes out of business. The FDIC will need to trace the investment through the bank and the broker to you before they agree to replace your money.

Liberty bonds were first issued in 1917 to help pay for World War I.

Bond,
SAVINGS BOND

The United States savings bonds that we know today have been around since 1935. US Treasury Secretary Henry Morgenthau Jr. wanted to get more people interested in investing in the US government. The idea of savings bonds wasn't a new one. Bonds had been sold in this country since the American Revolution. These bonds were marketable securities. This means that their value went up and down with the changing economy. The new bonds would be a safer investment. Morgenthau hoped that this would attract more investors.

During World War I, the government sold Liberty Bonds. Many of the people who bought these securities lost money a short time later. The economy was very poor during this period. People who needed money were forced to cash their bonds in when the value was less than what they had paid. Savings bonds issued after 1935 offered fixed interest rates. They had a guaranteed date when they would reach maturity. They could also be cashed in after a short

CHAPTER 4

INVESTOR TRIVIA

The United States government began issuing Patriot Bonds on December 11, 2001—three months to the day of the September 11 attacks. Although the bonds had a different name, they worked the same way as the Series EE bond.

waiting period without losing any of the principal investment. The government also began keeping records of who was purchasing the new bonds. If a bond was lost or destroyed, it could now be replaced.

Many people called the first of the new bonds "Baby Bonds." They were released in four series between 1935 and 1941: A, B, C, and D. Investors could buy Baby Bonds in denominations between $25 and $1,000. Each bond cost 75 percent of its face value. A $100 Baby Bond, for example, cost $75. It would then earn 2.9 percent interest each year as long as the owner kept it for the full ten-year period. About $4 billion worth of these bonds were sold during this six-year period.

The next bond that was introduced was the Series E bond. Until 1945, it was often called the "War Bond" because it helped pay for the expenses of World War II. The Series E savings bond became even more popular than previous series. It was promoted by many influential people and institutions. Bankers, newspaper publishers, and even famous actors and actresses encouraged Americans to buy Series E bonds. During the time they were available, more of these bonds were owned than any other type of security in the world.

Unlike Baby Bonds, Series E bonds kept earning interest long after they reached maturity. Depending on when a person bought one of these bonds, it could keep growing in value for thirty to forty years. Series E bonds were sold until 1980. The last of them kept earning interest until 2010.

"you buy 'em we'll fly 'em!"

DEFENSE BONDS STAMPS

THE MORE BONDS YOU BUY - THE MORE PLANES WE'LL FLY

The government sold savings bonds once again during World War II. The series E bond quickly became known as the "War Bond" for this reason.

Series EE savings bonds have featured the images of numerous US presidents—including Herbert Hoover, Franklin Roosevelt, Harry Truman, and Dwight Eisenhower.

The Series EE bond replaced the Series E bond. Very few changes came with this new series. The biggest change was that people could now use Series EE bonds to pay for certain higher education costs without having to pay taxes on the interest. If the total of the principal and the interest earned was higher than the amount used for education, however, the owner would be required to pay taxes on a percentage of the interest. People who made an especially high amount of money would also have to pay taxes on the interest, even if they used it for education.

Other series have come and gone over the years, but the only ones that are still being sold are the Series EE and Series I bonds. Series I bonds became available in 1998. In 2002 this series became a bit of a trailblazer, because investors could now purchase it online from the TreasuryDirect website at www.treasurydirect.gov. The following year, the government began selling Series EE bonds this way as well. If you have paper bonds that were purchased before this change, you can convert them to electronic bonds without suffering any penalties. Once you do, you can also monitor their progress online.

The differences between Series EE and Series I bonds are minimal. Both types are considered very safe investments. You have a slightly larger potential for growth with Series I, but you also have a slightly higher risk. These bonds have a variable rate of interest, which changes every six months based on the current inflation rate. Series EE, though, offers a fixed rate. It may be lower than what you will earn with a Series I bond, but you will know exactly how much money you will make the day you invest your money. Both series are now sold at face value. This means that a $100 savings bond now costs $100. Instead of being worth $100 at maturity, however, it will earn interest on top of the initial $100 value.

Savings bonds are designed to be long-term investments. You can redeem Series I bonds after the first twelve months of ownership, but you will pay a penalty for doing so within the first five years. Although you will lose your last three months' worth of interest, you won't lose any of your principal. If you think that you may need your money within the first five years, it could be smarter to put your money in a short-term investment, such as a CD.

Treasury bonds are a completely different investment from savings bonds. The owners of these bonds receive interest payments every six months until the bonds reach full maturity after thirty years. At maturity, the owner receives the face value of the bond. In addition to thirty-year

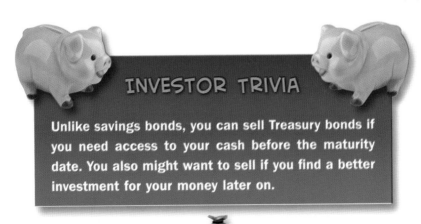

INVESTOR TRIVIA

Unlike savings bonds, you can sell Treasury bonds if you need access to your cash before the maturity date. You also might want to sell if you find a better investment for your money later on.

bonds, Treasury notes and bills are available for shorter terms. Treasury notes can be purchased with terms between two and ten years, while Treasury bills are available for terms of one year or less. Treasury bills do not pay out interest every six months; the total is paid at maturity instead.

Like savings bonds, Treasury bonds, notes, and bills can be bought at TreasuryDirect. You can also purchase these investments from banks and brokers. What really makes these investments different is that they are sold at auction.

Let's say you decide to purchase a Treasury bond. First, you must decide if you want a competitive or a noncompetitive bond. Most individual investors opt for the noncompetitive option, because all winning bidders receive the same interest rate, or yield, regardless of their bid type. Competitive bids must be placed through a bank or broker, and are usually placed by investors with large amounts of money.

During the competitive bid process, the investor asks for a specific yield. Competitive bidders may or may not receive the bond they want at the interest rate they want. The government offers a certain dollar amount of bonds, and will award them to the bidders who are willing to take the lowest yield. They continue to award bonds to bidders asking for a higher yield until all the bonds are taken. If the yield you want is higher than the yield established at the auction, your bid may be rejected. If your bid is equal to the yield from the auction, your bid may be accepted, but you may only receive a fraction of the bonds you wanted. If your bid is less than the yield chosen at auction, your bid may be accepted in the full amount. Everyone who receives a bond is given the highest yield that is accepted at that auction.

Noncompetitive bids are much simpler. These can be placed through a bank, broker, or through TreasuryDirect. In this case, you agree to accept the yield that is chosen at auction. Your yield may be lower than you'd like, but you are guaranteed to get a bond in the

Buying bonds can be a very confusing experience. Make sure you understand all the details before purchasing one of these investments.

amount you want. The yield may also come in at the amount you want or even higher.

Treasury bonds, notes, and bills are held as electronic accounts. At one time, though, they were issued on paper, like savings bonds once were. Like savings bonds, paper Treasury bonds can be converted into electronic form. Treasury bonds, notes, and bills have a minimum purchase amount of $100, and they are available in increments of $100. For example, you could purchase a Treasury bond for $300 or $400, but not $350. An investor can buy up to $5 million in noncompetitive bonds, notes, or bills per auction. But for competitive bidders, the maximum amount per investor is 35 percent of the total amount of securities up for bid at a single auction. Investors who want to invest more than $5 million usually place bids in competitive auctions for this reason.

Treasury bonds, notes, and bills are very safe investments, but it is important to consider the risks they do carry. If you put a large amount of money in treasury bonds when interest rates are low, you will receive far less interest on your money than someone who buys when the rates go up. On the other hand, if rates drop after you buy your bond, you will make out very well compared to other investors.

The secret to building a large nest egg for retirement is starting as early as possible.

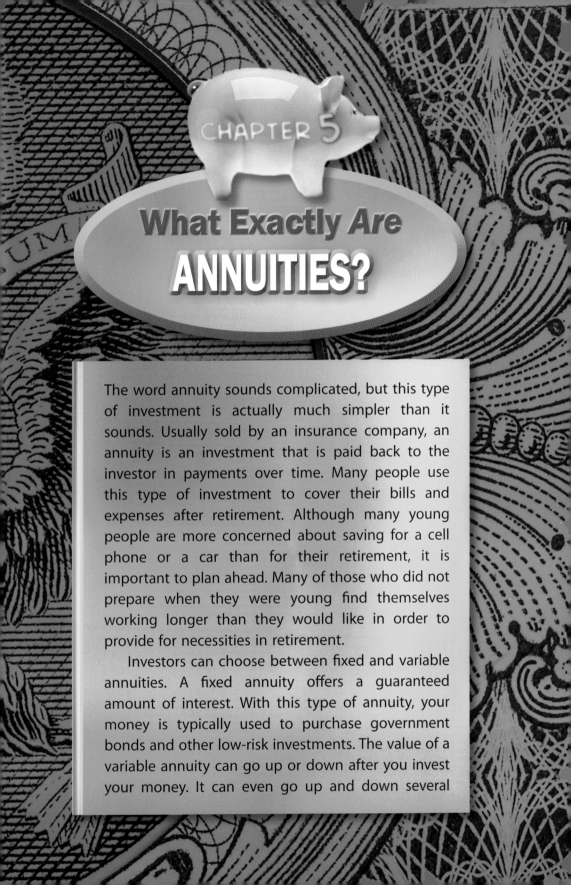

What Exactly Are ANNUITIES?

The word annuity sounds complicated, but this type of investment is actually much simpler than it sounds. Usually sold by an insurance company, an annuity is an investment that is paid back to the investor in payments over time. Many people use this type of investment to cover their bills and expenses after retirement. Although many young people are more concerned about saving for a cell phone or a car than for their retirement, it is important to plan ahead. Many of those who did not prepare when they were young find themselves working longer than they would like in order to provide for necessities in retirement.

Investors can choose between fixed and variable annuities. A fixed annuity offers a guaranteed amount of interest. With this type of annuity, your money is typically used to purchase government bonds and other low-risk investments. The value of a variable annuity can go up or down after you invest your money. It can even go up and down several times. This type of annuity puts your money into stocks and other higher-risk investments.

People who are close to retirement can opt for immediate payments on their annuities. Everyone else must choose annuities with deferred payments. You can begin collecting payments when you reach the age of 59 ½. Until then, you won't have to pay any taxes on the money earned from annuities. You can opt for payments that you receive for the rest of your life or payments that only go on for a certain period of time.

Both options include a certain amount of risk. If you opt for payments for life and you die before you receive all the money, the insurance company gets to keep whatever is left. If, however, you live long enough to collect all the money, you still will continue to receive payments from the company for the rest of your years.

INVESTOR TRIVIA

The word *yield* can be easy to confuse with interest. Although sometimes the two are the same, the yield can also refer to money earned that is not interest, such as dividends paid from investment in a stock. Also, interest rates are often compounded—meaning they are calculated at regular intervals, and then added to your principal. When this happens, you begin to earn interest on the interest, not just your original principal. So, the amount you earn at the end of the year (your yield), could actually be higher than your interest rate.

On the other hand, if you choose a set time limit for your payments and you die before you receive all of them, your beneficiary will receive the remaining payments. But if you are depending on the payments to cover your expenses, you run the risk of having to live many years without those payments.

Like many investments, annuities include certain fees. Many people think that the high fees many owners have to pay make annuities poor investments. The biggest advantage to an annuity is that it is an easy way to set aside a large amount of money rather quickly. Unlike other types of retirement savings, annuities have no limits on how much money you can put into them each year. You also won't have to pay any taxes on the earnings until you start collecting payments. People who are close to retiring often find annuities extremely helpful in these ways, especially if they haven't put away as much money for retirement as they would like.

For young people, the biggest benefit to buying annuities is the potential for growth. The money you invest will continue to increase over time and you won't have to pay taxes on your earnings until you withdraw them. If your fees aren't too steep, the compound interest you earn between now and your retirement could make this a worthwhile investment. Each annuity is different, though, so it is very important to read all the fine print before investing your money in one.

Variable annuities carry the biggest risks, but they also offer the biggest potential for growth. Fixed annuities are extremely safe investments as long as you don't need early access to your cash. If you must cash your annuity out before you turn 59 ½, you will pay a penalty whether the rate was fixed or not. The amount of the penalty depends on how long you have had the investment and the exact type of annuity you choose. No matter what, you will have to pay a tax penalty to the Internal Revenue Service (IRS) for early withdrawal. Expect to pay 10 percent of the amount that was earned in the account. In addition to this tax penalty, you may also lose about 7 percent of the value if you cash the annuity in within the first year. If you wait until

Saving just a small amount of money regularly can help you grow your savings in a big way over time. You might be surprised by just how much money your safe-haven investments add up to in the future.

the second year, you may only have to pay a 6 percent penalty. If you have had the annuity long enough, you may not have to pay any penalty at all. In this case, you will simply lose the interest that the investment would have made in the future.

The best types of savings are the ones that will pay you the most in interest and cost you the least in fees. The best investment today may not be the best one tomorrow. No one can see into the future, of course, but planning ahead is the key to making the best possible long-term decisions. The biggest risk lies in guessing which investments will be the most productive over time. But by keeping a good amount of your money in safe-haven savings, you can ensure that your money is both secure and earning more money, no matter which type of investments you choose.

INVESTMENTS TO EXPLORE

Here are some investing options you can explore if you are not up to taking any risks with your savings.

INVESTMENT
Statement Savings Account—Use this investment to earn a small amount of interest on your short-term savings as you add to your savings. Once your balance reaches a certain amount (such as $500), move all but $100 into one of the investment types below.
Certificate of Deposit—If you are new to this type of investment, you may want to start with a shorter-term CD (such as a six-month time deposit). Once it matures, you can then decide if you would like to buy another CD for a longer term (such as twelve months).
Savings Bonds—Instead of purchasing a single savings bond for $300, consider buying three $100 bonds, or six $50 bonds. Spreading your investment out this way will keep penalties low if you need to cash one of them in unexpectedly.
Treasury Notes and Bills—You might want to put $100 into a noncompetitive Treasury bill, and another $100 into a noncompetitive Treasury note. It will be interesting to see what yield you receive on these investments. You can then use this information when deciding whether you want to put more money into either type of investment in the future.
Fixed Annuities—You have a long time for this investment to grow. Since rates are so low right now, though, you might want to start small. The time to add more money to this type of investment is when rates rise.

Butler, Tamsen. *The Complete Guide to Personal Finance: For Teenagers.* Ocala, Florida: Atlantic Publishing Group, 2010.

Chatzky, Jean. *Not Your Parents' Money Book.* New York: Simon & Schuster Books for Young Readers, 2010.

Gardner, David, Tom Gardner, and Selena Maranjian. *The Motley Fool Investment Guide for Teens.* New York: Fireside, 2002.

Karchut, Wesley. *Money and Teens: Savvy Money Skills.* Colorado Springs, Colorado: Copper Square Studios, 2012.

On the Internet

FDIC. "Special Edition for Young Adults and Teens: Quick Tips for Managing Your Money." *FDIC Consumer News*, Fall 2012.

http://www.fdic.gov/consumers/consumer/news/cnfall12/Fall2012.pdf

SmartyPig

https://www.smartypig.com/

TreasuryDirect

http://www.treasurydirect.gov/tdhome.htm

Belz, Adam. "SmartyPig Creates Online Savings Plan To Reach A Goal." *USA Today*, July 26, 2012. http://usatoday30.usatoday.com/money/economy/story/2012-07-22/smartypig-social-money-michael-ferrari-jon-gaskell/56369606/1

Bruzzese, David, and Joshua Holmberg. *The Teen's Guide to Personal Finance.* New York: iUniverse, 2008.

Butler, Tamsen. *The Complete Guide to Personal Finance: For Teenagers.* Ocala, Florida: Atlantic Publishing Group, 2010.

Calonia, Jennifer. "The Death of the Certificate of Deposit: Will CD Rates Ever Rebound?" *U.S. News,* May 23, 2012. http://money.usnews.com/money/blogs/my-money/2012/05/23/the-death-of-the-certificate-of-deposit-will-cd-rates-ever-rebound

FDIC. "Your Insured Deposits." http://www.fdic.gov/deposit/deposits/insured/basics.html

Federal Reserve Bank of New York. "Certificates of Deposit." *Monthly Review,* June 1963. http://www.newyorkfed.org/research/monthly_review/1963_pdf/06_1_63.pdf

Fuscaldo, Donna. "Switch From a Bank to a Credit Union?" Bankrate.com, November 2, 2012. http://www.bankrate.com/finance/credit-unions/switch-from-bank-to-credit-union.aspx#slide=1

PBS, "Jesse James' Bank Robberies." American Experience. http://www.pbs.org/wgbh/americanexperience/features/general-article/james-robberies/

TreasuryDirect. http://www.treasurydirect.gov/tdhome.htm

Wang, Jim. "5 Reasons Credit Unions Rock." Bankrate.com, June 9, 2011. http://www.bankrate.com/financing/banking/5-reasons-credit-unions-rock/

asset (AS-et): something that is owned and has value

beneficiary (ben-uh-FISH-ee-er-ee): the person who receives money or property when another person dies

broker (BROH-ker): a person or company that buys and sells investments on behalf of others

defer (dih-FUR): to postpone or delay until a certain time in the future

denomination (dih-nom-uh-NEY-shun): one in a series of different values

high yield (HAYH YEELD): paying a higher rate of return than most other investments of the same type

inflation (in-FLEY-shuhn): the rise of prices and the decrease in the value of money

interest (IN-ter-ist): payment for the use of another's money

maintenance fee (MEYN-tuh-nuhns FEE): the amount of money charged to an investor by a bank or other financial institution for managing an investment

mature (muh-CHOOR): to become due for repayment

penalty (PEN-el-tee): the loss of a sum of money for breaking the terms of an account or investment

principal (PRIN-sih-puhl): the original amount of money placed in an investment; separate from interest other money earned from the investment

quarterly (KWAWR-ter-lee): every three months

security (sih-KYOOR-ih-tee): any of a number of types of investments

term (TURM): a set time period

yield (YEELD): the amount of money earned on a investment

Index

About the
AUTHOR

Tammy Gagne has authored more than seventy-five books for both adults and children over the last decade. She has been investing for twice this time. In addition to managing her own portfolio, she has taught her teenage son about the details of his investments, enabling him to make some of his own decisions in this area. She believes that young people should know how money works, so their money can work for them instead of vice versa. When young people understand investing and feel in control of their finances, they get excited about money. They also tend to have more of it.